First Facts®

OUR PLACE IN THE UNIVERSE

EARTH AND OTHER PLANETS

by Ellen Labrecque

CAPSTONE PRESS
a capstone imprint

First Facts is published by Capstone
1710 Roe Crest Drive, North Mankato, Minnesota 56003
www.mycapstone.com

Copyright © 2020 by Pebble, a Capstone imprint. All rights reserved. No part of this publication may be reproduced in whole or in part, or stored in a retrieval system, or transmitted in any form or by any means, electronic, mechanical, photocopying, recording, or otherwise, without written permission of the publisher.

Library of Congress Cataloging-in-Publication Data

Names: Labrecque, Ellen, author.
Title: Earth and other planets / by Ellen Labrecque.
Description: North Mankato, Minnesota : Pebble, a Capstone imprint, [2020] |
    Series: First facts. Our place in the universe | Audience: Ages 6-9. | Audience:
    K to grade 3. | Includes bibliographical references and index.
Identifiers: LCCN 2018054589| ISBN 9781977108487 (hardcover) | ISBN
    9781977110183 (pbk.) | ISBN 9781977108654 (ebook pdf)
Subjects:LCSH: Planets--Juvenile literature. | Earth (Planet)--Juvenile
    literature. | Solar system--Juvenile literature.
Classification: LCC QB602 .L2325 2020 | DDC 525--dc23
LC record available at https://lccn.loc.gov/2018054589

Editorial Credits

Hank Musolf, editor; Kyle Grenz, designer; Jo Miller, media researcher; Kathy McColley, production specialist

Photo Credits

NASA, 13 (Both); NASA/JPL, 12; Newscom: BSIP/JACOPIN, 15, Cover Images/NASA, 19; Shutterstock: Aphelleon, 7, 22, Christos Georghiou, 5, Macrovector, 11, MarcelClemens, Cover (Earth), Robert P Horton, 21, Romolo Tavani, 8, Sunti, 9, Vadim Sadovski, Cover (Planets), 16 (All), 17
Design Elements
Capstone; Shutterstock: Alex Mit, Dimonika, Kanate

All internet sites appearing in back matter were available and accurate when this book was sent to press.

Printed and bound in China.
1671

Table of Contents

Meet the Planets

How many planets are there in the **universe**? So many that we can't count them all! A planet is a large, round object. It **orbits** around a star.

The solar system is in the universe. The solar system includes a huge star, the sun. It also includes the eight planets that travel around it. Our planet, Earth, is one of these eight. Let's learn about Earth and its planet neighbors.

orbit—to travel around an object in space

universe—everything that exists, including the Earth, the planets, the stars, and all of space

Venus

Mercury

Saturn

Mars

Earth

Uranus

Jupiter

Neptune

5

Home Sweet Home

Earth and the other planets get their light from our star, the sun. Planets spin as they orbit. When one side of the Earth turns away from the sun, it is night there. When it turns toward the sun, it becomes day. It takes 24 hours for the Earth to make one full turn.

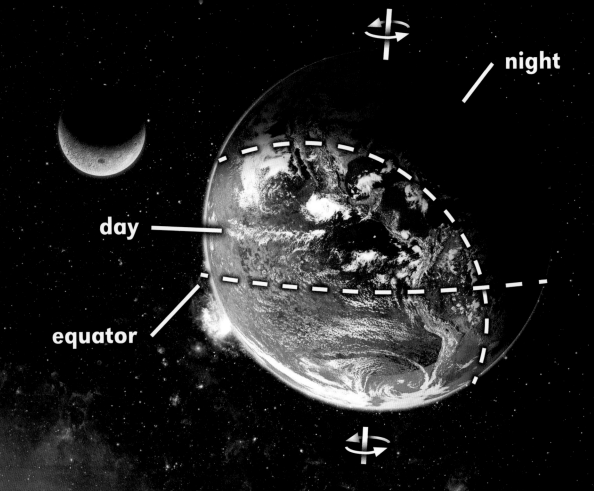

night

day

equator

FAR-OUT FACT

Long ago, planets were called wandering stars.

Take a deep breath. The air is just right for us to breathe. Earth is the perfect planet for life. It is not too cold or too hot. It has plenty of water.

Earth is the only planet **scientists** know of that has life on it. But the universe is big. It has so many other planets! Do you think there is life on another planet?

scientist—a person who studies the world around us

You can look at stars and other planets with a telescope.

Earth's Neighbors

The four planets of Mercury, Venus, Earth, and Mars are like neighbors. They are called the inner planets. They are closest to the sun. These four are also called the rocky planets. They formed in a cloud of dust and gas. Heat helped form them into rocky balls. They are made up mostly of rock and metal.

FAR-OUT FACT

Most of the planets are
named after Roman gods.

Mars

Mercury

Earth

Venus

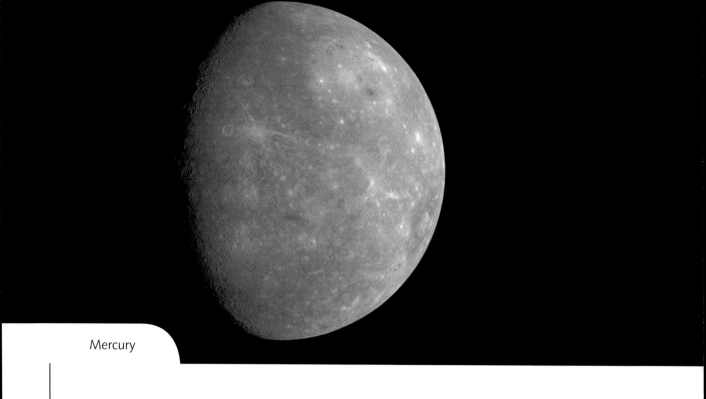

Mercury

Mercury and Venus are the two
planets closet to the sun. Mercury
is the smallest and fastest planet
in the solar system. It zips
around the orbit path. It takes
88 days for it to circle the sun.

Venus is the hottest planet. It is hot enough there to melt metal! Mars is the most like Earth. It has a red tint to it. It is called the red planet.

FAR-OUT FACT

Rovers are unmanned robots with wheels. They have already explored Mars.

Mission to Mars

Soon people will likely travel to Mars. A company called SpaceX hopes to put people there by 2030. The trip would take about nine months. People would always have to wear space suits there. They couldn't breathe without them.

The Giant Planets

Jupiter, Saturn, Uranus, and Neptune are the biggest planets in the solar system. The only object bigger than Jupiter is the sun. These four are called the outer planets.

They are farthest from the sun. They are made up mostly of gas. This means a spacecraft could never land on one of them. They are only solid at their core.

Asteroid's Belt

A belt lies between the inner and outer planets. But it is not the kind of belt you wear around your waist. This belt is the **asteroid** belt. Asteroids are like smaller planets. Close to 2 million asteroids are in the asteroid belt.

asteroid—a rocky object in space

asteroid belt

Imagine if all of the asteroids were put together into a ball. They would still be smaller than the Earth's moon.

Uranus

The outer planets are far away from the sun. We could not survive in their freezing temperatures. Uranus and Neptune are nicknamed the ice giants.

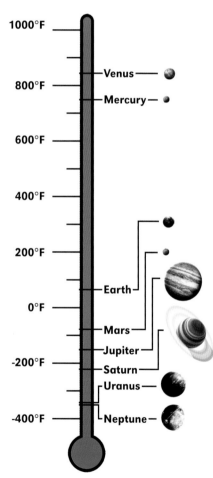

Temperatures of Planets

1000°F	
800°F	Venus
	Mercury
600°F	
400°F	
200°F	
0°F	Earth
	Mars
	Jupiter
-200°F	Saturn
	Uranus
-400°F	Neptune

The outer planets have rings around them made of ice, dust, and rocks. Saturn has four groups of rings. They are made of ice.

FAR-OUT FACT

The outer planets have more than 140 moons between them. Jupiter has 67. Saturn has more than 60. Uranus has 27. Neptune has 14.

Neptune

Planets around Other Stars

An exoplanet is a planet outside of our solar system. These planets are far away from Earth. No one knows how many of these planets exist. We can't even see them with a **telescope**. We have seen some of them using **satellites**. Satellites are objects that people send up in space. They take photographs and collect data for us.

satellite—a spacecraft that circles Earth; satellites gather and send information to Earth

telescope—a tool that makes faraway things look closer than they are

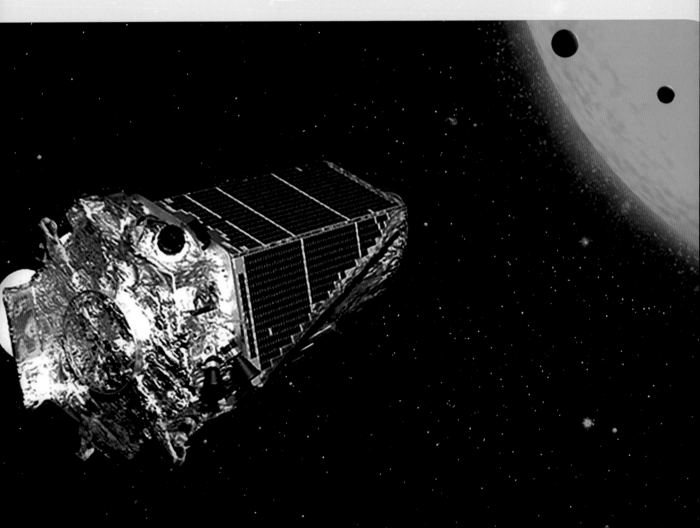

FAR-OUT FACT

The closest exoplanet to Earth is very far away. It would take us hundreds of years to get there.

Look Up!

Don't forget to look up when you are outside at night. You'll see lots of stars and the moon. On some nights, some of the brightest stars are actually planets! Keep exploring space on your own! What you can learn is truly out of this world!

Venus

Moon

Jupiter

Glossary

asteroid (AS-tuh-roid)—a rocky object in space

orbit (AWR-bit)— to travel around an object in space

satellite (SAT-uh-lite)—a spacecraft that circles Earth; satellites gather and send information to Earth

scientist (SYE-un-tist)—an expert in the field of science

telescope (TEL-uh-skope)—a tool that makes faraway things look closer than they are

universe (YOO-nuh-vurs)—everything that exists, including the Earth, the planets, the stars, and all of space

Read More

Bell, Samantha. *Solar System.* North Mankato, MN.: Cherry Lake Publishing, 2018.

DK. *First Space Encyclopedia.* My World of Science. DK First Reference. New York: Penguin Random House, 2016.

Internet Sites

NASA Kids' Club
https://www.nasa.gov/kidsclub/index.html

National Geographic Kids: Passport to Space
https://kids.nationalgeographic.com/explore/space/passport-to-space/

Critical Thinking Questions

- If you could travel to Mars, would you go? Why or why not?

- Which planet is the hottest?

- How many days would it take for Earth to orbit the sun if it orbited at the same speed as Mercury? How would this make life on Earth different?

Index